The Fly on the Wall

PHASE 5

5a

Level 5 – Green

Helpful Hints for Reading at Home

The graphemes (written letters) and phonemes (units of sound) used throughout this series are aligned with Letters and Sounds. This offers a consistent approach to learning whether reading at home or in the classroom. Books levelled as 'a' are an introduction to this band. Readers can advance to 'b' where graphemes are consolidated and further graphemes are introduced.

HERE IS A LIST OF NEW GRAPHEMES FOR THIS PHASE OF LEARNING. AN EXAMPLE OF THE PRONUNCIATION CAN BE FOUND IN BRACKETS.

Phase 5			
ay (day)	ou (out)	ie (tie)	ea (eat)
oy (boy)	ir (girl)	ue (blue)	aw (saw)
wh (when)	ph (photo)	ew (new)	oe (toe)
au (Paul)	a_e (make)	e_e (these)	i_e (like)
o_e (home)	u_e (rule)		

HERE ARE SOME WORDS WHICH YOUR CHILD MAY FIND TRICKY.

Phase 5 Tricky Words			
oh	their	people	Mr
Mrs	looked	called	asked
could			

HERE ARE SOME WORDS THAT MIGHT NOT YET BE FULLY DECODABLE.

Challenge Words			
officer	cheese	fly	swat

TOP TIPS FOR HELPING YOUR CHILD TO READ:

• Allow children time to break down unfamiliar words into units of sound and then encourage children to string these sounds together to create the word.

• Encourage your child to point out any focus phonics when they are used.

• Read through the book more than once to grow confidence.

• Ask simple questions about the text to assess understanding.

• Encourage children to use illustrations as prompts.

PHASE 5

5a

This book is an 'a' level and is a green level 5 book band.

The Fly on the Wall

Written by
William Anthony

Illustrated by
Emre Karacan

"We will get them, James," said Officer Willis. James ran Velvet Cheese. It was a small pizza shop in Junktown.

Last night, someone had taken all of the pizzas.
"Thank you for your help, Officer Willis. The Junktown Pizza-Fest is just two days away!" said James.

The Pizza-Fest was a clash of the best pizzas in Junktown.

Velvet Cheese and Cheesus Crust were the best. Kids and adults would come from far away to eat the pizzas.

The cops needed to act fast to help James and Velvet Cheese get to the Pizza-Fest.

Officer Willis had a plan. He planted a bug at Velvet Cheese. But this was not a normal bug...

"I'm Officer Vic. How can I help?"
The small fly said as she held up her card.
"James was robbed," said Officer Willis.

"But the Pizza-Fest is in just two days! I'm on it!" Vic yelled. Off she buzzed.

"What person would want James out of the Pizza-Fest?" Vic had a think and gasped, "Harper!"

Harper ran Cheesus Crust. It all added up! If James had no pizzas, she would win.

Vic buzzed off to Cheesus Crust. She landed on the wall. Harper was out.

She spotted a stack of pizzas. Were they from James' shop? She buzzed over to look.

"Oh no! Fly! Get off my pizzas!" Harper was back. She grabbed a box and tried to swat Vic.

Harper just missed. Vic buzzed off and went back to see Officer Willis.

Willis had something red on his shirt.
"It's just jam," he said. "Have you got
the pizzas yet?"

"No, but I have a suspect. I went to see Harper and she tried to swat me!" said Vic.

Vic tried to buzz off, but got her leg stuck in a cobweb on the wall.
"At last, it's just me," said Willis.

He jumped up and pulled out a box.
"Wait a second..." Vic muttered. Willis
took a big chomp of cheese.

"I'll rob Harper's pizzas next and then I'll win the Pizza-Fest!" he said to himself. Vic pulled free and called for backup.

"Officer Willis! You are under arrest!"
she yelled.
"Am I?" asked Willis. He put a glass on Vic.

Vic jolted from left to right. She was
stuck.
"STOP RIGHT THERE!"
Vic's backup burst into the room!

Officer Tom let Vic out of the glass. She sat on his hand.
"Good job, Officer Vic," said Tom.

The cops took Willis and put him in the prison van. Vic went to tell James.

James was sat with Harper. "I'm glad you got Willis, but I still have no pizzas," he told Vic.

"Just for this Pizza-Fest, maybe we can cook together?" asked Harper. "We can call our pizza stall the Velvet Crust!"

James and Harper cooked the best pizzas ever.
"This pizza is for you, Vic. I'll never swat you again!" said Harper. Vic winked.

The Fly on the Wall

1. What was the name of the two pizza shops which were always in the final of Pizza-Fest?

2. What did Harper try to do to Vic?
   (a) Make her fly out of the window
   (b) Trap her under a glass
   (c) Swat her away

3. Did you think it was jam on Willis' shirt? What else did you think it could have been?

4. What did Willis do to Vic to stop her arresting him?

5. Do you think Harper was right to offer to work together with James? What would you have done if you were Harper?

©2020 **BookLife Publishing Ltd.**
King's Lynn, Norfolk PE30 4LS

ISBN 978–1–83927–297–4

All rights reserved. Printed in Malaysia.
A catalogue record for this book is available
from the British Library.

The Fly on the Wall
Written by William Anthony
Illustrated by Emre Karacan

An Introduction to BookLife Readers...

Our Readers have been specifically created in line with the London Institute of Education's approach to book banding and are phonetically decodable and ordered to support each phase of the Letters and Sounds document.

Each book has been created to provide the best possible reading and learning experience. Our aim is to share our love of books with children, providing both emerging readers and prolific page–turners with beautiful books that are guaranteed to provoke interest and learning, regardless of ability.

BOOK BAND GRADED using the Institute of Education's approach to levelling.

PHONETICALLY DECODABLE supporting each phase of Letters and Sounds.

EXERCISES AND QUESTIONS to offer reinforcement and to ascertain comprehension.

BEAUTIFULLY ILLUSTRATED to inspire and provoke engagement, providing a variety of styles for the reader to enjoy whilst reading through the series.

AUTHOR INSIGHT:
WILLIAM ANTHONY

Despite his young age, William Anthony's involvement with children's education is quite extensive. He has written over 60 titles with BookLife Publishing so far, across a wide range of subjects. William graduated from Cardiff University with a 1st Class BA (Hons) in Journalism, Media and Culture, creating an app and a TV series, among other things, during his time there.

William Anthony has also produced work for the Prince's Trust, a charity created by HRH The Prince of Wales, that helps young people with their professional future. He has created animated videos for a children's education company that works closely with the charity.

PHASE 5

5a

This book is an 'a' level and is a green level 5 book band.